THE FALL OF CONSTANTINOPLE

The Brutal End of the Byzantine Empire

Written by Romain Parmentier
In collaboration with Gauthier Godart
Translated by Carly Probert

History 50MINUTES.com

THE FALL OF CONSTANTINOPLE

KEY INFORMATION

- **When:** 6 April-29 May 1453
- **Where:** In Constantinople, the capital of the Byzantine Empire (now Istanbul)
- **Context:** The Ottoman expansion (14th - 17th century)
- **Belligerents:** The Byzantine Empire against the Ottoman Empire
- **Commanders and leaders:**
  - Constantine XI, Byzantine emperor (1403-1453)
  - Mehmet II, Sultan of the Ottoman Empire (1432-1481)
- **Outcome:** Ottoman victory
- **Victims:**
  - Byzantine camp: approximately 4 000 dead and 50 000 taken prisoner
  - Ottoman camp: figure unknown, but losses were significant

INTRODUCTION

A major turning point in European history, the fall of Constantinople marked the end of the Eastern Roman Empire (commonly called the Byzantine Empire) in favor of the Ottoman Empire. According to many historians, this event precipitated the end of the Middle Ages and marked the entry of Western Europe into modern times.

The fight for Constantinople began on 6 April 1453. The attack was ordered by the Ottoman Sultan Mehmet II, who wanted to bring an end to the Byzantine presence on the Bosphorus. The stakes were high: taking possession of Constantinople would not only ensure the control of commercial links between the East and the West, but would also end the last Christian stronghold in the East. The Ottomans, aware of this issue, therefore undertook the siege of the city, seeking to seize it by progressively weakening it through a series of offensive attacks, but also through a blockade intending to isolate and deprive it of any external help.

The Byzantine Empire that tried to resist the attack was declining. Behind the impressive ramparts of Constantinople, the emperor Constantine XI managed to keep the Turks at bay for more than 50 days. Nevertheless, given the successive assaults, the city finally fell on 29 May 1453, sealing the fate of the two Empires, marking the end of the Byzantine Empire and the dawn of the Ottoman Empire.

POLITICAL AND SOCIAL CONTEXT

BYZANTIUM: AN EMPIRE IN AGONY

A milestone in the history of the 15th century, the fall of Constantinople was only the final act of a process of a centuries-long decline for the Byzantine Empire. Since the fall of the Roman Empire in 476 A.D., which marked its advent, nearly a thousand years passed, during which the empire was maintained, despite the claims that some (such as the Arabs, Serbs, Bulgarians, Venetians, Genoese and Turks) had on its territories.

> ### GOOD TO KNOW
>
> For some historians, the birth of the Byzantine Empire occurred in 395 A.D. when Emperor Theodosius I (347-395) decided to share the Roman Empire between his sons. Although several divisions had already been made in the past, this was definitive. However, it was primarily administrative and the inhabitants of the two empires did not perceive any real differences compared to the previous situation. For example, they were subject to the same legislation. It was not until 476 A.D. that the Byzantine Empire conducted its own destiny.

The decline of the Byzantine Empire began in 1204, when the Republic of Venice, for reasons of commercial competition, redirected the Fourth Crusade (1201-1204), which was originally headed for Constantinople, towards the re-conquest of the Holy Land and Jerusalem, then under the control of the Arabs. This event, which was rooted in the religious quarrel between the Churches of the East and the West since the schism of 1054, would have devastating consequences. The Byzantine capital was indeed besieged and conquered by the Crusaders who ransacked it, signaling the end of the Byzantine Empire, which then broke up into four entities:

- the Latin Empire of Constantinople (1204-1261), which included Thrace, northwestern Minor Asia, Lesbos, Samos and Chios, and was in the hands of Westerners;
- the Despotate of Epirus (1204-1318), located in the Balkans and extending to Albania and Greece;
- the Empire of Nicaea (1204-1261), located along the Sea of Marmara and the Black Sea, led by the Emperor Theodore I Laskaris (c. 1174-1222);
- the Empire of Trebizond (1204-1461), located in the Pont region, on the coast of the Black Sea, which was one of the last refuges of the Greeks before falling into the hands of the Ottomans in 1461.

However, in 1261, Michael VIII Palaiologos (1224-1282), co-emperor of Nicaea then Byzantine emperor, managed to reclaim Constantinople and restore the Byzantine Empire. The damage caused by the Crusaders however proved irreversible, leading to the final break between the two Churches.

THE TURBAN, RATHER THAN THE MITER

In the 14th century, the Byzantine Empire, already weakened by a disastrous economic situation, was undermined by incessant succession struggles. The empire was now limited to Europe only. Meanwhile, a new power was emerging: the Ottomans. They gradually monopolized the remaining Byzantine territories, so much so that at the beginning of the 15th century, all that remained of the empire was Constantinople and the Morea (Peloponnese). At the height of humiliation, to ensure its survival, it was forced to pay a tribute to the invader, reducing Byzantine emperors to vassals of the Ottoman Empire. The city of Constantinople, meanwhile, lost its splendor and gradually depopulated.

Faced with the Ottoman threat, several emperors tried to gain help from the West. However, religious issues were always at the center of negotiations and Rome required the union of the Eastern Church with that of the West as a prerequisite for any form of assistance. This prerogative was at the heart of the councils of Ferrara and Florence which, in 1438 and 1439, tried – in vain – to achieve the union of the two Churches. Backed into a corner, the last Byzantine emperors were forced to accept this compromise, causing the growing discontent of the population, which was permanently marked by the atrocities committed by the Crusaders in 1204: the union agreements were consequently seen as real treason. It was in this context of tension that the Grand Duke Loukas Notaras, high admiral of the Byzantine fleet (died in 1453) would have said the famous quote: "I would rather see a Turkish turban in the midst of the City than the Latin miter" (Nicol 1993).

In 1444, the Christian world began a final crusade to counter the Ottomans, but this ended in failure at the Battle of Varna.

GOOD TO KNOW

The Battle of Varna took place on 10 November 1444, and was fought between Sultan Murad II (1404-1451) and the Christians led by John Hunyadi (military man and politician from Transylvania, 1387-1456), King Vladislav I of Hungary (1423-1444) and Prince Vlad Dracul of Wallachia (1397-1447), father of the count that inspired the novel *Dracula* by Bram Stoker).

Faced with the increasingly urgent threat of the Ottomans on Constantinople and the Balkans, Pope Eugene IV (1383-1447) ordered the preparation of a new crusade against the Muslims.

The Crusaders began to move in July 1444 and planned to reach the port of Varna in order to board ships to Constantinople. However, the Christian fleet was delayed, allowing the Sultan Marnad II to send his army to Varna. On 10 November, the two armies met and engaged in combat. Although the advantage seemed to be with the Crusaders, the young king Vladislav I began a miscalculated offensive which cost him his life and threw confusion into the Western army. The consequences were terrible: the Hungarian monarch was killed, John Hunyadi was put to flight and the Christian army was virtually annihilated. The Ottoman Sultan therefore won the battle, ending the crusade and depriving Constantinople of any reinforcement, which would prove decisive when taking the Byzantine capital a few years later.

THE RISE OF THE OTTOMAN EMPIRE

Whereas the Byzantine Empire had existed for centuries, the Ottoman Empire was born in 1299. Its founder, Gazi Osman I (c. 1258-1326), and his successors continued to increase their power and expand their territory. In 1354, the Ottomans seized land located in Europe, such as the city of Gallipoli. From then on, it was no longer possible to impede their advance which continued in the Balkans, especially with the conquest of Adrianople by the third Ottoman Sultan Murad I (1326-1389) in 1362.

This left no more than 200 kilometers to reach Constantinople, which was still in the hands of an already moribund Byzantine Empire. However, it would take another few decades for the city to fall. The reason for this delay was not due to a possible weakness of the Ottomans. Indeed, the Ottomans were facing multiple threats that prevented them from conquering Constantinople: the Serbs and the Christians in the West, the Mongols in the East and the succession struggles between Sultans constantly delayed the conquest of the Byzantine capital. For example, one can consider the enterprise of Sultan Murad II, who, while he besieged Constantinople in 1422, was recalled because of a rebellion in Anatolia, bringing an abrupt end to the siege. Nevertheless, the situation changed with the succession to power of Mehmed II.

CONSTANTINOPLE: THE DREAM OF MEHMET II

On his accession to the throne of the Ottoman Empire in 1451, Mehmet II had only one goal: to take Constantinople and end up with the Byzantine Empire. Indeed, the Ottoman Sultan measured the stakes of such a conquest. This would enable him to:

- connect the European and Asian parts of the Ottoman Empire;

- create a bridge to the Balkans and other conquests;
- control the Bosphorus Strait, of crucial importance from a commercial and military standpoint;
- obtain international recognition;
- destroy the Byzantine Empire and end the Christian authority in the East.

Mehmet II intended to stack the odds in his favor to avoid a similar failure to that of 1422. His plan of attack was carefully prepared during the two years preceding his victory.

Eager to counter any external threat, the Sultan began by renewing peace treaties with his Christian and Muslim vassals. He then proceeded to deprive Constantinople of any chance of rescue by cutting it off from its possible auxiliaries. To do this, Mehmet II signed a treaty with the Republic of Venice in September 1451 and, in November, concluded a three-year peace with John Hunyadi, representative of the Kingdom of Hungary.

From 1452, the Sultan also launched military diversions in the Morea, which was then in the hands of the brothers of Constantine XI, to prevent them from rescuing the capital at the time of the siege. Therefore, all that remained was for Mehmet II to completely isolate Constantinople by establishing a blockade of the city on the Bosphorus. To this end, the Sultan built the castle of Rumeli Hisari north of the strait, in front of another Ottoman fortress built by one of his predecessors, Bayezid I (c. 1360-1403). With these two fortresses he now controlled the north of the strait, preventing any ship from the Black Sea from supplying Constantinople. In November 1452, Venetian ships loaded with wheat, attempting to break the blockade, were sunk by artillerymen sheltered by the fortresses. Everything was now in place for the siege of Constantinople, the thirtieth and last in its history.

COMMANDERS AND LEADERS

CONSTANTINE XI PALAIOLOGOS, BYZANTINE EMPEROR

Constantine XI Palaiologos, nicknamed Dragases (1403-1453), was the last Roman emperor of the East who witnessed the fall of Constantinople. The younger son of Emperor Manuel II (1348-1425), Constantine XI was not destined to reign on the throne of Byzantium. Therefore, when in 1421, Manuel II became wearied by years of conflict, he appointed his eldest son, John VIII (1390-1448) co-emperor. It was in this capacity that John VIII undertook a first trip to the West in 1423-1424, to find help in facing the Ottoman threat that was becoming increasingly urgent. The young Constantine XI Palaiologos, responsible for the regency of the empire during his brother's absence, became a despot (the highest title in the imperial ranks).

In 1425, following the death of Manuel II, John VIII became the only reigning emperor. He attributed to three of his brothers (Constantine XI, Theodore and Thomas) the government of the Morea, the latest stable province of the empire. Constantine XI Palaiologos became despot of Morea at Vostitza from 1427 to 1437, before returning as regent of the empire from 1437 to 1440 during a new voyage of his brother to the West, undertaken to end the religious disputes and facilitate the preparation of a new crusade against the Ottomans. Upon the emperor's return, Constantine XI Palaiologos resumed his role as despot of Morea. However, a change occurred in 1443 when he offered the city of Selymbria to his brother in exchange for Mistra (city of Morea). Although he continued to lead the province together with his brother Thomas, he now held the richest and most extensive part of the Morea.

The fate of Constantine XI switched in 1448, when his brother John VIII died. The latter having no heir, the throne of Constantinople fell to him. On 6 January 1449, he was thus crowned *basileus* (title designating Byzantine Emperor). But the honor of this title was accompanied by many responsibilities, including facing the Ottomans. However, the situation was desperate: the enemy had succeeded over time, in surrounding what remained of the empire. Therefore, Constantine XI was forced in turn to claim the support of the Western powers. He obtained this support, but it came at a price: indeed, he was obligated to proclaim the union and the submission of the Eastern Church to the Roman papacy in 1452, much to the dissatisfaction of the population of Constantinople. This ultimate concession of the Byzantine Empire remained ineffective: no help would come from Rome in 1453.

Meanwhile, Sultan Mehmet II had resolved to end the Byzantine Empire. In April 1453, the Byzantine capital was under siege. Despite the lack of manpower at his disposal, Constantine XI organized the defense of the city and closed the Golden Horn (the natural port of Constantinople) with a long chain. He also served as head of 3 000 men to defend the city wall at the Gate of Saint Romanus. This was followed by 55 days of resistance. Before the final attack on 29 May 1453, Mehmet II offered Constantine XI the sovereignty of the Morea in exchange for the surrender of the city, but the emperor refused and replied that he was ready to sacrifice his life rather than surrender. This decision sealed his fate, as well as that of Constantinople, and the Turkish onslaught proved insurmountable. Followed by a few faithful men, Constantine XI launched into the fray with his sword and suffered a heroic death, ending the long line of Roman emperors. His body was never found.

MEHMET II, SULTAN OF THE OTTOMAN EMPIRE

Mehmet II (or Mehmed II), the seventh Sultan of the Ottoman Empire, was the instigator of the siege of Constantinople in 1453. The son of Sultan Murad II, he ascended to the Ottoman throne in 1444, when he was only 12 years old. The reasons that prompted his father to abdicate in favor of his son are still a mystery. However, the youth of the new Sultan had one major drawback: the growing influence of his teachers on the government of the empire eventually arose the opposition of the great leaders, the most famous of which was Halil Pasha (grand vizier of the Ottoman Empire in 1439-1453), as well as the army. Murad II was therefore called back to the throne in 1446, ending the first reign of Mehmet II.

In 1451, the death of his father prompted his second accession to power. The five years between his two reigns allowed the young Sultan to complete his education and also to be initiated into military and state affairs. Mehmet II was now ready and had only one objective: to permanently get rid of

Constantinople, in order to succeed where his father had failed in 1422. Yet the young sultan did not launch into an ill-prepared siege, but rather the contrary. For two years, he gradually isolated Constantinople to prevent any rescue when the time came for the siege. It was not until April 1453 that he began the siege of the Byzantine capital, which he took possession of at the end of May. From then on, Constantinople became the capital of the Ottoman Empire and Mehmed II was nicknamed Mehmed the Conqueror.

Mehmed II's conquests did not end there. Strengthened by the knowledge of his victory, the Sultan decided to annex Serbia permanently to his empire. From 1454, he began the conquest of this territory until the siege of Belgrade in 1456. The campaign nevertheless ended in failure. The Ottomans would have to wait three years to finally take full possession of Serbia. Mehmed II then worked to seize the last vestiges of the Byzantine Empire in 1461 by defeating the Despotate of Morea and the Empire of Trebizond. Two years later it was the turn of Bosnia to be submitted, followed by Albania in 1467. The Balkans was now in the possession of the Ottoman Empire. Genoese and Venetian counters located on the shores of the western Mediterranean and the Black Sea were also gradually conquered by the Sultan, and Crimea was subjugated.

Mehmet II led conquests and campaigns until the end of his life, increasing the power and size of his empire. He died in 1481 at the age of 49 as a result of poisoning, according to certain sources.

ANALYSIS OF THE BATTLE

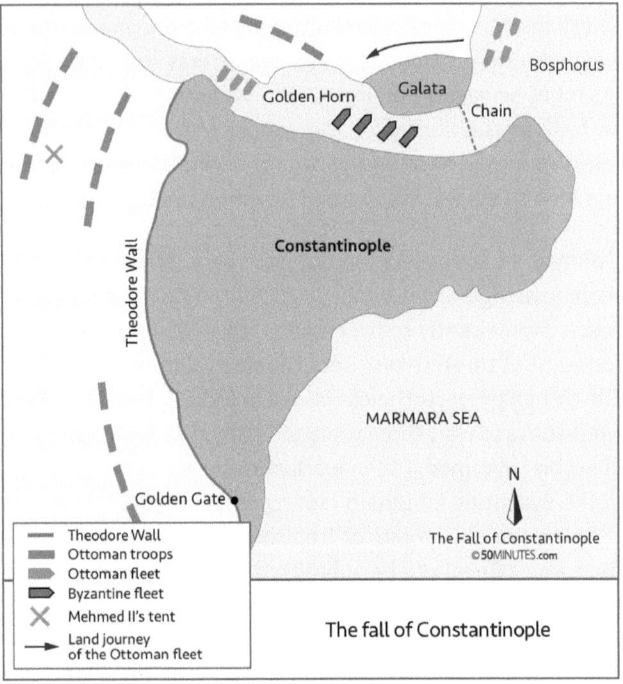

The fall of Constantinople

PREPARATIONS

To achieve his objective, Mehmet II spent several months preparing the isolation of Constantinople. It was now time to gather his army. Therefore, the Sultan mobilized all the contingents available to him, as well as those due to him by his vassals. In total, approximately 80 000 soldiers gathered under the banner of the Sultan, including 10 000 Janissaries, the elite infantry of Mehmet II. The Sultan also possessed, with more than 100 ships, the largest naval fleet ever assembled by the Ottomans. Nevertheless, it was his artillery that would make all the difference in the siege: in fact, this was the first time that it was used in such large numbers. Fourteen batteries, each containing four big guns, were positioned facing the wall, the centerpiece of this structure being the Orban barrel (named after the Hungarian engineer who designed it, died in 1453), which became famous for its impressive dimensions (eight meters long) and its ability to send cannonballs of 600 kilos – a technical feat for the time. It took no less than 200 soldiers and 60 oxen to transport it to Constantinople. Its goal was to destroy the ancient city walls.

Faced with this colossal army, the situation in Constantinople seemed even more desperate. Abandoned by the West, the city could only rely on its few soldiers and some foreign auxiliary quotas. In his writings, Georges Phrantzes (1401-1478), adviser and historian to Constantine XI, mentions 4973 men able to fight, including monks and clergymen. Added to this were 2 000 to 3 000 foreign soldiers, mainly from Venice and Genoa, whose most famous contingent was that of Genoese Captain Giovanni Giustiniani Longo (c. 1418-1453), which contained 700 men. In total, there were between 7 000 and 8 000 men who were set up to defend Constantinople and were, for the most part, assigned to the defense of the city wall, against which the attacks would be charged. As for the naval defense, the city was equally as helpless as it only had 25 warships to defend the Golden

Horn. Finally, weaponry was also insufficient: the soldiers were fighting with cold weapons, and artillery of the city was virtually obsolete.

However, despite its limited resources, Constantinople had two significant defensive devices. To understand the importance of this, it is vital to remember that, geographically, the city formed a triangle on the Bosphorus: in the north was the Golden Horn, to the south was the Marmara Sea and to the west was the inland wall. These devices were:

- The chain that closed the port of the Golden Horn, connecting the tower Eugene (located on the ramparts of the city) to the walls of the fortress of Galata, which was on the other side. The chain, which rested on wood floaters and was defended by nine warships, prevented other ships from entering the Golden Horn. No frontline could therefore be opened from this side, allowing the defenders of the city to have troops in other areas.
- The fortified walls of Theodosius II (Emperor of the East, 401-450) were composed of three lines of defense. It stretched over seven kilometers and protected the inland side of the city. To reach the city, attackers must first pass an 18-meter wide ditch of six to nine meters in depth, which was followed by a slope. They would then reach the outer wall which was protected by towers of ten meters in height placed every 50-100 meters. Finally, they still needed to pass the inside wall (12 meters high), which had 96 towers that were 18 meters tall. This device was therefore vital for the inhabitants of Constantinople, who strengthened it on the eve of the battle.

The Byzantines were also fully aware of the projects of Mehmet II. In February 1453, the army of the Sultan had already taken possession of the countryside and the outskirts of Constantinople. From 2 April, the troops arrived in front of the city and faced the ramparts. Three days later, they were joined by the Sultan: the entire Ottoman army was in position. As for the Emperor Constantine XI, he distributed the defense troops: the battle for Constantinople could begin.

THE HOPE AMIDST THE FIRING

On 6 April 1453, Mehmet II launched attacks and ordered the bombardment of the walls of Constantinople. This systematic shelling became a daily occurrence throughout the duration of the siege. The Orban cannon then revealed its true power and, although it could only be fired seven times a day, its cannonballs inflicted serious damage to the walls of Constantinople. Gaps were formed in the walls and towers were sprayed. After a few days, thanks to the canons of reinforcements of more modest dimensions, the monster artillery brought down an entire section of the wall. However, the Orban barrel exploded, killing its creator at the same time. Meanwhile, the Sultan ordered his soldiers to bridge the ditch between them and the outer wall, in order to best prepare the onslaught of the infantry. Out at sea, the struggle was hard: the Ottoman fleet was trying to break the chain of the Golden Horn.

For the inhabitants of Constantinople, the incessant noise of the guns quickly became an ordeal. This was also mixed with the sound of drums and cymbals destined to prevent the defenders from resting. It was a true psychological warfare that began in Constantinople. However, the defenders did not lose hope and even won several successes:

- The Ottoman fleet was continually thwarted before the chain of the Golden Horn;
- The breaches made by the Ottoman artillery in the wall

were filled during the night;

- Ditches were re-dug to the point where, every morning, the Sultan's soldiers were forced to start their labor anew.

On 18 April, judging that the damage to the wall was sufficient to launch an attack, Mehmet II first made an attack with his infantry, but this was repelled by the Byzantines. From their rampart, they used Greek fire against the Ottomans, an incendiary weapon which only they knew of. The gates of the city were brilliantly defended by Giovanni Giustiniani Longo. This small victory allowed the Byzantines to regain confidence. This sense of hope was reinforced on 20 April when three Genoese ships and an important imperial battleship emerged on the waters of Constantinople with soldiers, food and ammunition on board. Mehmet II immediately ordered their destruction in vain; at night, these four ships faced the Ottoman fleet alone and managed to enter the Golden Horn, which bowed its string especially for the occasion. The Sultan, furious at this new failure, dismissed his admiral.

DID YOU KNOW?

Greek fire is an incendiary weapon based on saltpeter and bitumen that was used by the Byzantines. Even today, we can only speculate as to its exact composition. This weapon was able burn on water, and was therefore often used during naval battles. It was also used as grenades or clay barrels, catapulted to defend the cities. Finally, using pumps, Greek fire could be projected directly at the enemy like a flamethrower.

THE FEAT OF THE GOLDEN HORN

Humiliated, Mehmet II had only one obsession: to enter the Golden Horn. However, the chain did not waiver. It was in this context that the most improbable operation of the battle took place. The Sultan decided to transport a part of his fleet overland, bypassing the fortress of Galata in front of the slide in the Golden Horn, in order to attack the Byzantine fleet from behind. On the night of 22-23 April 1453, 70 smaller vessels were out of the water and hoisted onto huge wagons pulled by oxen over a distance of 1.3km. This gigantic operation required thousands of men, but it was a success: at daybreak, the inhabitants of Constantinople, horrified, saw the Ottoman fleet descend gently into the channel of the Golden Horn.

Through this feat, Mehmet II opened a new front to the city, forcing the already sparse defenders to spread over a much wider area. The Ottoman artillery was immediately fired against the walls, in order to open new breaches. On 28 April, the Byzantines tried anyway to destroy the fleet entering the Golden Horn, namely by sending incendiary ships to oppose it. However, the Ottomans managed to repel them: the Byzantine operation ended in failure. But although Mehmet II opened a second front, the situation of his ships in the Golden Horn was far from favorable. Indeed, they were stuck in the port by the chain that remained in place throughout the duration of the siege, despite multiple attempts to destroy it. The casualties at sea were numerous. Meanwhile, the bombardment of the walls continued while the besieged people began to weaken and the reserves were running out.

The battle raged on land and sea, but also underground. Mehmet II ordered some soldiers to dig mines to join the walls in several places and place explosives to bring down the wall. The operation was dangerous and the risk of collapse was high, but victory was to be gained at any cost. Having understood the plans of the Ottomans, the Byzantines strived to build more mines until 25 May to destroy those dug by their opponents: the operation of Mehmet II ended in failure once again. On 18 May, the Sultan tried a new attack and hoped to climb the walls with a huge wooden tower placed on wheels, but this was burned before it reached the wall.

From either side of the ramparts, morale was gradually declining: the Byzantine reserves were almost exhausted, the expected reinforcements from Venice did not arrive, it was becoming increasingly difficult to fill the holes in the wall, and some events, such as a lunar eclipse, were viewed as bad omens. The Ottomans were also exhausted by the siege that did not seem to be coming to an end and their successive failures. Faced with this situation, Mehmet II then offered Constantine XI the possibility of a capitulation, but the Byzantine emperor stated that he would rather die than give up Constantinople. The end was near.

THE FINAL ATTACK

After a council of war, Mehmet II ordered the intensification of the bombing of the ramparts throughout the day of 27 May. When a part of the interior wall collapsed, the Ottomans felt hopeful again: they now had the means needed to take Constantinople. The following day, the Sultan granted a day of rest to his soldiers in preparation for the final attack. On the Byzantine side, it was clear that the end of the battle was near. The paintings and relics were taken out of the churches and walked around the city walls. Residents gathered at the Saint Sophia Basilica, putting aside their religious quarrels to share one last Mass together. Emperor Constantine XI, after seeking absolution for his sins, went to the walls to encourage his troops one last time.

The Capture of Constantinople, painting by Tintoret, 1580.

The final attack began on 29 May 1453, at around 1:30am. The first wave of Ottoman soldiers swept the inland wall of Constantinople, supported by artillery and the sound of drums. The attack was focused on a gap in the wall, which was ardently defended by the men of Giovanni Giustiniani Longo. For hours, the Ottoman troops were pushed back, but immediately replaced by new troops. The Sultan wanted to leave no respite to the Byzantines until they were completely exhausted. He then sent the Janissaries, his elite troops.

At dawn, the fighting continued, but Giovanni Giustiniani Longo, who would undoubtedly be remembered as the greatest defender of Constantinople, was wounded and evacuated from the battlefield. His departure weakened the resistance terribly and despair overcame the Byzantines. The Janissaries took this opportunity to deliver the final blow: climbing the city walls, the eventually reached a tower, at the top of which they planted the Ottoman flag. Encouraged by this spectacle, the soldiers charged at the walls and eventually broke the Byzantine forces and entered the city through a hole located near the gate of Adrianople. Constantine XI, who defended the Gate of Saint Romanus, then engaged in a final fight with a few faithful soldiers: this was the last time the emperor would be seen.

The Fall of Constantinople, illustration from "Hutchinson's History of Nations", 1915.

Becoming more and more numerous in the city, the Ottomans gradually opened all doors: now, the city belonged to them and was ransacked. Desperate, the last defenders of the city returned to their homes to protect their families. Furthermore, the chain of the Golden Horn was broken, allowing the Ottoman fleet to take possession of the port at around noon. As for the Venetians and the Genoese, they were forced to leave the city.

The human losses were significant in the siege, but no exact figure has been established; only the figures of 4 000 Byzantine casualties and 50 000 prisoners are widely accepted.

After 55 days of siege, Constantinople finally surrendered, falling into the hands of Sultan Mehmet II, but many authors salute the courage of the Byzantine garrison for having stood so long in the face of the Ottomans' overwhelming numerical superiority.

REPERCUSSIONS OF THE BATTLE

A CITY TRANSFORMED FOREVER

As soon as the Ottoman victory was assured, the soldiers and the Janissaries of the Sultan subjected the city to the ransacking, looting and massacre of the Byzantines that they found in their path. The patrimony of the city also suffered the worst abuses: religious paintings were desecrated and broken into pieces and the Saint Sophia Basilica, where part of the population fled, was looted of its wealth. The Sultan's entrance to Constantinople ended the massacre. To seal his victory, Mehmed II went to the basilica, the spiritual heart of the city, and granted clemency to the inhabitants who had survived. The building was then converted into a mosque, ending centuries of Christianity in Constantinople. Despite the granting of freedom of worship as soon as 1453, Christians today make up no more than 2% of the city's population.

Picture of the inside of the Saint Sophia Basilica taken in 1909.

Over the years, the face of Constantinople was gradually transformed. Mehmet II first began to repopulate the deserted city and made it the capital of his new empire. Ancient churches were equipped with minarets, and new mosques were built in the city. Many typical buildings of Islamic civilization were built, such as baths and madrasas (Islamic schools). The only thing that remained of the ancient Byzantine capital was the ramparts and the Saint Sophia Basilica. Finally, the city was renamed Istanbul, before starting a new prosperous period under the yoke of the Ottoman emperor powers.

THE END OF THE BYZANTINE EMPIRE AND THE BEGINNING OF THE OTTOMAN GOLDEN AGE

Since the ransacking of Constantinople by the Crusaders in 1204, the Byzantine Empire gradually saw its power wane. The capture of the city in 1453 marked the culmination of this decline and the final collapse of the empire in favor of the Ottomans. Different Byzantine institutions were thus removed and the management of the population, territory and state was now operated according to the Ottoman model. Although Mehmet II granted religious freedom, the Orthodox heritage was transferred to Moscow, which became "the third Rome" for the Russian Orthodox Church.

Therefore, all that remained of the Byzantine civilization was the Despotate of Morea and the Independent Empire of Trebizond. However, neither entity could survive for very long as Mehmet II could not tolerate the existence of these shelters of the Hellenic nation which could potentially generate a new crusade against his empire. In 1453, the Despotate of Morea was owned by Thomas and Demetrius, the last two brothers of Constantine XI. Far from uniting in order to maintain the autonomy of their province, the two brothers kept fighting to increase their power. In 1458, Mehmet II discovered that they were both conspiring with Pope Pius II to lead the West in a new crusade. This prompted the Sultan to decide to invade a third of the Despotate of Morea, before ending it definitively in 1460. A year later, it was the turn of the Trebizond Empire to disappear, ending the Byzantine presence in the East.

However, beyond the death of an empire, it was also the birth of another that marked the fall of Constantinople. The Ottoman Empire had existed since 1299, but the fall of Constantinople ensured it a status as a new great power and marked the beginning of its golden age and its significant territorial expansion, in Europe, Africa and Asia. This expansion also began the gradual takeover of the Balkans by Mehmet II, as its control became increasingly important after the fall of Constantinople. The future indeed seemed well assured for the empire, which would extend to the gates of Vienna and only come to an end in 1923, during the official proclamation of the Turkish Republic.

The fall of Constantinople fulfilled the expectations of Mehmet II:

- Taking the city allowed him to connect the European and Asian parts of the empire, ensuring better communication between them;
- The Bosphorus Strait was now fully under his control, allowing him to control trade in this area, while being a strategic place from a military point of view;
- He could now present himself as heir of the Roman emperors and give his empire a new status of power that the West would have to deal with;
- Finally, the fall of Constantinople, and that of the last bastions of Byzantine civilization, put an end to the Crusades and guaranteed stability for the Ottoman Empire.

THE END OF THE MIDDLE AGES?

The year 1453, like the year 1492 (year of the discovery of America by Christopher Columbus), is often referred to as a key date in the transition of medieval Europe to modern times. Although the fall of Constantinople was a major event in European history, it would nevertheless be wrong to believe that the Middle Ages came to an abrupt end with the death of the last Byzantine emperor. This passage from one era to another is much more complex and is part of a long-term process that began long before the fall of Constantinople and continued long after.

However, the fall of Constantinople undeniably contributed to a significant change in attitudes which was crystallized under the name 'Renaissance'. Throughout its existence, the Byzantine Empire was home to many intellectual centers, the most important of which was Mistra in Morea. The breakup of the empire thus caused the flight of many scientists and scholars towards Western Europe, mainly to Italy, taking with them their knowledge, but also part of the Greco-Roman heritage that Byzantium had inherited. The arrival of these intellectuals therefore allowed Europeans to rediscover the Greek texts, a major source of inspiration for the Italian Renaissance.

Meanwhile, the fall of Constantinople had a direct impact on trade relations between the West and the East. Goods (silk, spices, incense, etc.) from the East, which were highly coveted in Europe, partly passed through Constantinople. However, the fall of the Byzantine capital and the resulting

Ottoman expansion resulted in higher taxes on goods, thereby slowing trade. Europeans would therefore launch to conquer new trade routes, leading them to great discoveries. The road to China being closed since the capture of Acre by the Muslims in 1291, the European powers would constantly seek a new way to reach China and India, skirting the African continent, as would the Portuguese, or by crossing the Atlantic, like Spain and France.

Although this maritime expansion already existed in a smaller form before the fall of Constantinople, particularly through the expeditions implemented by the Portuguese Prince Henry the Navigator (1394-1460), this experienced a huge boom as a result of the capture of the Byzantine capital, which decisively strengthened the need to find new sea routes, deeply transforming the relationships between different parts of the world.

SUMMARY

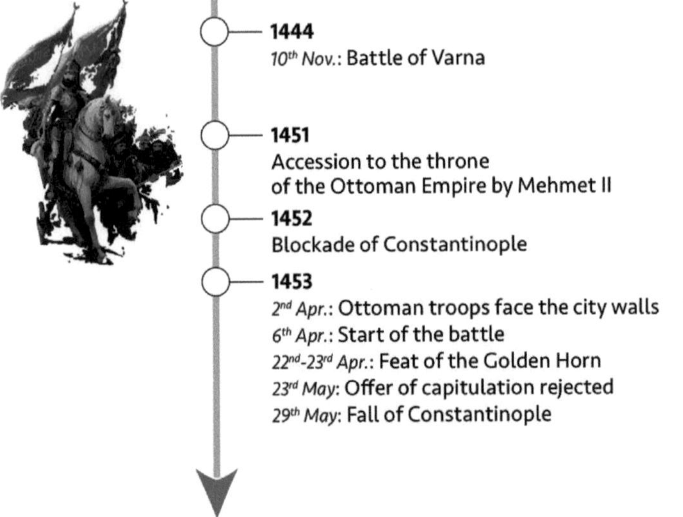

1444
10th Nov.: Battle of Varna

1451
Accession to the throne
of the Ottoman Empire by Mehmet II

1452
Blockade of Constantinople

1453
2nd Apr.: Ottoman troops face the city walls
6th Apr.: Start of the battle
22nd-23rd Apr.: Feat of the Golden Horn
23rd May: Offer of capitulation rejected
29th May: Fall of Constantinople

- On the decline for several centuries, the Byzantine Empire was limited to the capital and the Morea by the 15th century. In 1449, Constantine XI became emperor and was the last bastion against the Ottoman expansion.
- In 1451, the Ottoman Sultan Mehmet II came to power, with only one objective: to seize Constantinople. To completely isolate the city, the Sultan concluded treaties with Venice and Hungary.
- On 6 April 1453, he triggered hostilities by ordering the bombing of the walls of Constantinople.
- Following several military failures, the Ottoman army sent a part of its fleet by land during the night of 22-

23 April, in order to break into the Golden Horn, which was closed off by a chain, and to attack the Byzantine troops from behind. This achievement opened up a new front; the bombing of the Ottoman artillery then started all over again.

- On 23 May, Mehmet II offered Constantine XI an honorable capitulation, but he refused to give up Constantinople. Four days later, after a day of intensive bombing, a section of the inner city wall collapsed.
- On 29 May, the final attack was launched by the Ottomans at 1:30am, combing artillery and waves of infantry, but they were pushed back one after the other.
- At dawn, Giovanni Giustiniani Longo was wounded and evacuated from the battlefield, greatly weakening the Byzantine defense. Meanwhile, Constantine XI died with weapons in hand.
- In the course of the morning, the Ottomans finally managed to enter Constantinople through a breach near the gate of Adrianople.
- Around noon, the chain closing the Golden Horn was broken; the Ottoman fleet took possession of the port of Constantinople.
- In the evening, Mehmet II entered the city, ending the atrocities committed by his troops. He reached the Saint Sophia Basilica and granted clemency to the survivors.
- Over the years, Constantinople was transformed by the adoption of Ottoman customs. Now all that remains of the Byzantine capital is the walls and the basilica.

We want to hear from you!
Leave a comment on your online library
and share your favourite books on social media!

FIND OUT MORE

BIBLIOGRAPHY

- Babinger, F. (1992) *Mehmed the Conquerer and His Time.* New Jersey: Princeton University Press.
- Bréhier, L. (2006) *Vie et mort de Byzance.* Paris: Albin Michel.
- Laiou, A. and Morrisson, C. (2011) *Le monde byzantin. III. L'Empire grec et ses voisins.* XIIIe-XVe *siècle.* Paris: Presses Universitaires de France.
- L'avancée des Turcs dans l'Europe des XVe et XVIe siècles (2007) *Histoire universelle. Le Bas Moyen Âge et la Renaissance,* Volume 11. Paris: Hachette.
- Malherbe, J. (2001) *Constantin IX. Dernier empereur des Romains.* Louvain-la-Neuve: Academia-Bruylant.
- McCarthy, J. (1997) *The Ottoman Turks: An Introductory History to 1923.* London: Longman.
- Nicol, D.M. (1993) *The Last Centuries of Byzantium: 1261-1453.* Cambridge: Cambridge University Press.
- Schlumberger, G. (1914) *Le Siège, la Prise et le Sac de Constantinople par les Turcs en 1453.* Paris: Plon-Nourrit.

ADDITIONAL SOURCES

- Crowley, R. (2013) *Constantinople: The Last Great Siege, 1453.* London: Faber and Faber Limited.
- Harris, J. (2016) *The Lost World of Byzantium.* New Haven: Yale University Press.
- Herrin, J. (2008) *Byzantium: The Surprising Life of a Medieval Empire.* London: Penguin.

- Runciman, S. (2012) *The Fall of Constantinople 1453*. Cambridge: Cambridge University Press.

ICONOGRAPHIC SOURCES

- *The Capture of Constantinople*, painting by Iacopo Robusti, known as Tintoret (Italian painter, 1518-1594), 16th century, exhibited at the Doge's Palace in Venice. Royalty-free reproduction image.
- *The Fall of Constantinople*, illustration taken from "Hutchinson's History of Nations", 1915. Royalty-free reproduction image.
- Picture of the inside of the Saint Sophia Basilica taken in 1909. Royalty-free reproduction image.

FILMS AND DOCUMENTARIES

- *L'Ascension de l'Empire ottoman.* (2012) [Documentary]. Melissa Akdogan, Nick Gillan-Smith, John Fothergill and Jack MacInnes. Dir. Part of the *De l'Orient à l'Occident* series. USA.
- *Constantinople* (2013) [Film]. Faruk Aksoy. Dir. Turkey: Aksoy Film, Medyapim.

MUSEUMS AND COMMEMORATIVE BUILDINGS

- The fortress of Rumeli Hisari (Istanbul).
- The Panorama 1453 history museum (Istanbul).
- The ramparts of Théodose II (Istanbul).
- The Galata tower (Istanbul).

50MINUTES.com
Business & Economics
History
ISHIKAWA DIAGRAM
Material Method Machine
Mother Nature Measure Men
Management & Marketing 50MINUTES.com
THE BATTLE OF AUSTERLITZ
ADAM SMITH
Livres